IN THE HOT-HOUSE

IN THE HOT-HOUSE
Alan Jenkins

Chatto & Windus   LONDON

Published in 1988 by
Chatto & Windus Ltd
30 Bedford Square
London WC1B 3RP

A CIP catalogue record for this book is available from the British Library

ISBN 0 7011 3312 0

Acknowledgements are due to the editors of the following publications in
which some of these poems first appeared: *Encounter*, the *New
Statesman*, the *Observer*, *Oxford Poetry*, the *Sunday Times*, the *Times
Literary Supplement*.

Photoset by Rowland Phototypesetting Ltd
Bury St Edmunds, Suffolk

Printed in Great Britain by
Redwood Burn Ltd
Trowbridge, Wilts

In memory of Donald F. Jenkins, 1916–1984

Contents

Feast

At a table in a fisherman's house in Sète
the fisherman's son and ten or twelve of us, his friends –
French and English, the Algerian girl – all sat
and opened oysters with our bare hands,

oysters from a barrel that was sprigged with seaweed,
bottomless, as though he had sunk a well
to a salt-water lake below the house, an oyster-bed.
I plunged in for another crusted shell

and it released the reek of seaweed and sea, reek of a girl.
The barrel stood as high as our chests
and the plates were stacked with mother-of-pearl.
I watched the black points of Khedidja's breasts

jiggling inside her shirt, and flushed with *apéros*
and *vin rosé*, I wanted to still them, so thought I'd try
to sit her on my lap like a powdered fop from Paris
in *Le déjeuner d'huîtres* by Jean François de Troy.

The Old Order

My grandfather had seen better days –
he did the round of lakeside hotels and roulette tables.
I loved his cardboard suitcase,
its leather corner-patches, art-deco labels.

Genoa, Lausanne, Biarritz –
he made a small fortune on each trip
but had spent it within weeks
of coming home. A passport and some ivory chips
his only relics.

At Grandmother's house for Sunday tea
I'd take them into a corner

on my own, or group them on the plush settee.
Grandmother always seemed to be in mourning

like her furniture and plants,
but sinking in an armchair
she smiled indulgently as I strafed the chintz.
Smells of lavender and mothballs filled the air
and a row of long-dead great-aunts,

embalmed in sepia, glared down
from their oval frames; but the palm,
the tiny splash of blue and sun-bleached town
on his card, intimated something warmer.

At sixteen or seventeen
I slept in the corridor of a train and woke between
pink and yellow-painted villas,
vineyards, hills like aubergines,
olive-groves and bougainvillaea –

my grandfather, so I was told,
never really grew up.
He lived for fun, as dice and Pullmans rolled
across the green baize of Europe.

Privacy

'Going out' meant lying in a green-laced tent
together, lacerated by the floor
of twigs and insects – the frown you wore
as we picked straws from each other's clothes and hair;
going back, the sunset-reddened evening air,
the crushed, drooping stems, our bodies' print
on the wind-combed sea of bracken . . .

One night, in zip-joined sleeping bags
after a party, we looked up at peeling
plaster, cornices like a wedding-cake –
winds shook the hallway, flake on flake
came spiralling down to us, flat on our backs –
and saw the great mirror in the ceiling
that had held this strange couple's twinned
contortions, a trapped snake
coiling and struggling. I imagined
the fierce eyes, the tense grin
crouched behind it.

              At last we put real tents
above the sea, among the scents
of eucalyptus, pine. I watched you dive,
wearing only *la petite culotte* – so thin,
it showed a smudge of shadow at your groin
when you surfaced, blurry-brown, a blonde's;
I heard your unhurried plash and ripple,
glimpsed an upturned breast and bead-like nipple,
your shoulders' web of scars, the filaments
connecting you to your element –
then I saw him, furtive, ducking
cypress-branches for a better view.
The air was a breath-held hush, a troubled haze.
Underwater, under curling fronds
of light, the weeds you threaded were mined
with urchins – all spikes and purplish-dark,
swollen, stiff-haired parts . . . Broken,
halved on marble slabs or high and dry
on rocks, each one is a gaping eye,
a perfect, blank, wide gaze.

Guardian

She turned up in a holy terror of a dream,
when he was next in line for the drop
down some pit of helplessness or shame.
The hour when hearts can stop.

He soon knew her by her smells, her sap.
Where he sprawled, mosquitoes primed a blaze
at mid-day in the stricken maize,
cicadas went off like a trap

or something wired. A cart trailed by, a dust-cloud.
Rustling poplars whispered to him out loud:
Come. Leave the fusty velvet, the suffocating palms
of the parlour, and mother's outstretched arms.
Leave your damp pillow, your hard bed.
Come now. Here is my terracotta, my Etruscan red.

(Once, in a park, he'd watched two men embrace.
But as for thrones and powers, cherubim and seraphim,
he'd never held with it. No angel had come near him.)

Here are my raw siennas, my burnt umbers.

The Introduction

Three men pause a moment in the dazzling air
at the top of the steps.
All three are smiling, as if
for a photograph
you would have taken, had you been there.
One of them stands slightly apart,
at a not quite formal distance.
It is your father.
He introduces the others:
'Mr Foster, this is Mr Cavafy.'

Then, still wearing their awkward smiles,
they go down to the dazzling garden.

It is perfect, the table and the fountains,
the patch of shade
where two men sit
in white crumpled suits,
at their slight angle to things, which takes in, between sips,
the boy who brings them lemonade.
It is like nearby Eden,
or a total eclipse
in the middle of the desert.
Your father has gone back inside the house
and watches from his study windows
something to do with history, or art,

or something that has nothing to do
with either,
as he now thinks,
his eyes fixed on the skyline of Alexandria.
And what was it
Flaubert said of the Sphinx?
Or was it perhaps the pyramid?
The plump, forbidden fruits
would sweat it out as Nile slid by,
the flies would dance their seven veils
above the heads of those two in the cool penumbra,
mouthing the difficult words, their eyes perfectly happy.

In the Hot-house

Tropical fir-trees, tendril-trails
of liana,
locked in together, have their fun.

A cathedral that's wet and warm!
Loudspeakers fill our ears
with the shrieking of children and birds,

a steady murmuring of prayer.
There's a nasty storm
but it's still Paradise. The kind of air

you'd expect to find in Guiana,
the drenched fronds
of palm and fern, a thousand of our closest friends.

The Grand Duke's window. Poisonous snails.
Boxwood sleeping in the sun.
The hose-pipe's coils. You're lost for words.

Language Lessons

My tongue in your mouth, one hand in the Biba vest
and firmly on your breast,
the other sliding through a scratchy mulch inside your
    tights . . .
(A room where perpetual dusk
had fallen on the things from India, where musk
and patchouli warred with marijuana, incense,
where someone sobbed about a stairway to heaven
or sang 'I've come from Brooklyn to study astrology',
'Happiness is a warm gun', 'I feel free'
and 'Brighton girls are like the moon'.)

Then: the park long after closing, a clump
of long grass. Your legs tightening their clasp,
my hip grinding hard into your cleft, and *Wait.*
Not yet, oh fuck, not yet – a clenched rasp . . .
I thought of you, hearing the words *dry hump.*
I remembered your breast in stark moonlight,
a smooth white stone coming clear of your blouse,
its network of pale purples, blues.

   *

A camp-site terrace and its vine-chinky shade.
After lunch I put down *The Portrait of a Lady,*
left you sleeping in a heat-heavy tent
and followed a deserted, winding trail
that kept losing and finding itself as it went
on up the mountain like a lizard's tail . . .

By now I have come just far enough
to see, looking back down the same path
in the instant between two cars
one afternoon in Rome – the time, near enough,
it would take a lizard's eyelid to open and close
or Henry James to strike out a clause –
the salt-drifts on your nape, a tiny Sahara,
your nipples puckering the water-tautened cloth.

The same scratchy soundtrack, a sarabande
echoing after ten years in a shaded house,
great windows open to the south,
a terrace on fire, a mountain with an S-bend,
the wicks of cypress turned right up –

   *

takes me back to teaching *jeunes filles en fleur,*
night-whispers through the wooden hive of the attic floor,
gin and orange for 'our little group',
Yeats one day, Robert Graves the next . . .

We clawed cockles from the sucking sand –
you chopped the garlic with a trembling hand,
I tried to keep my mind on the text . . .

You wore my shirt on an outing to somewhere
so that the others would know.
You were still wearing it weeks later, though now
at *notre petit nid d'amour au bord de la mer* –
I'd exchanged my touchy colleagues
for your feminist collective and philosopher-goatherds,
the palms bristled like disgruntled birds,
their feathers on fire, and armies of *cigales*
wound everyone up at night . . .

                             I skulked like a thief
between your parents, your brothers and you,
taking them all in as I took in the view
of beached, helpless fishing-boats, the Château d'If.

P.S.

Will write see you soon K.O.
on the postcard; *PS*
Hotel Esmerelda, Paris
or somewhere in the Mile End Road.
Then she herself, who hadn't showed
in over a year, would be sitting there
behind the wheel of her boyfriend's Cadillac,
trailing a cloud of patterned scarves
and a dog-eared Tolkien or Kerouac.

Not one to do anything by halves.
A T-shirt printed 'Little Stinker', the biggest Harley-
Davidson east of Long Island Sound.
She wrote once that she remembered
my second-hand boots 'in the middle of the carpet'
– they stayed there while we were in bed,
after much drinking and skirting the issue.

16

One night, appearing out of the blue
and eating her first square meal
in over a week, with her first square –
me – she took me back and offered to cast my nativity.
Over and over, she played Van Morrison's
Astral Weeks, and read the signs
in a cup of camomile tea.
She rolled joint after joint in her red-painted kitchen
then piled cushion on huge scatter-cushion
on the floor, and let me feel
how far her centre of gravity
had shifted from the ground.

A sacrificial fledgeling in its nest;
her shoulder-blade's constellation
of freckles; a single star in the curtainless window,
a star tattooed on her left breast.

The Old Tune

I was walking past a patch of waste ground
that doubled as front lawn and battlefield
for a block of council flats –
windows boarded, everything and everybody running
        riot –
when I heard them drifting from high up,
climbing higher, the clear notes
of a single phrase
played on an alto saxophone.
The sound made its own kind of quiet –
that rich pause before each stop.

These were the dog-days,
this was August, English summer-heat-wave heat.
The music knocked me off my feet
and blew my head away
to Paris, 1970:
a boy of fifteen
on my own for the first time in that city,
I'd been driven up and down the *quais*
by a student not much older than myself
I'd befriended on the Dunkirk train.

He fixed me up in a hotel
on one of the smarter streets in Passy.
The ironwork of the lift, the view of the Tour Eiffel
were nothing to what I saw and heard
one night, getting into bed –
from across the courtyard
came a tune played on the sax,
so sweet . . .
And in the window, a man's silhouette,
a girl swaying close, tuning up for sex.

I listened as it all went down.
I watched her giving head.
I carried that tune like a talisman.
And I've heard saxophonists since then
who've opened the world up wider
than Marlon Brando
Maria Schneider,
wider than the eyes of that girl in the window,
than even Belmondo
murmuring to no-one *Marianne, Marianne*.

Strange Days

Anyone who chanced to pass by in the street
and glance inside, that summer, would have seen
the two colour prints by Utamaro –
reproductions you'd cut from a magazine
and pinned up to fade in the heat.
But this was different. A man had come
when I wasn't there, and asked to have a closer look.
His eyes had feasted on our room,
on the dressing-table clutter, on each book,
on the piles of clothes and papers scattered
round the place we ate, slept, fought and made up in.
And, squinting as he lit a cigarette,
they had roamed across and lingered
on the creased, abandoned sheets;
then he'd said, 'D'you want to sell?
Name your price. I'll come back tomorrow.'

That was that. There was nothing more to tell.
Nor was there anything in your voice, the way
you told it, remotely like suspicion, or fear.
It seemed you simply had no idea
of the kind of people walking the streets –
There's more out than in, your mother used to say.
He could not have seen us more naked if
he'd come on us both in a book of cartoons
from the private library, or a Japanese
pillow book: the grinning courtesan,
the hairy old warlord, thicker, purpler, fatter
each time; flesh-tints, great folds of skin.
Or if he'd stood beside the bed and fingered
your kimono, gently, gently; caught a whiff
of musty, fraying silk, perfume and sweat,
then forced, you first, then me, to our knees.

Teeth

We ended up as we'd begun:
sitting on a bed in someone's house,
a party going on downstairs, between us
every kind of trouble –
an hour before, we'd gone against the grain
of the stripped-pine kitchen, our hosts' ifs and buts,
and were bent double
trying to get in touch. Our mouths wouldn't fit
on account of your two front teeth.
Every muscle felt the strain.
We finished in a heap on the floor,
nerve-ends holding out for more . . .
Then shared the mattress with another couple.
That night we were almost undone –
a pin-prick would have burst the bubble –
but all we exchanged were love-bites.

Now here we were again,
two different people
in another stranger's bedroom,
doing something . . . illicit.
I was like Miss Lonelyhearts,
dejected, down-at-heel, plucking at your nipple
with finger and thumb,
lifting the shirt off your back,
taking a free hand to your gusset . . .
This time what we did was nothing new –
until, that is, you said 'I only want
to hurt you, now', took me between your teeth
and bit. I couldn't see much point
in staying around to talk,
though I could see something in your point of view.
I took a deep breath and said 'It hurts.'

The Road Poem

There's your stylish socialite
who punishes a sports car
all the way to a party in the shires,
roaring back to the mews half-tight,
all squealing and exhaust, late on Sunday night,
smoke coming off his tyres . . .

I couldn't be the one who drives
a blonde to distraction down some leafy lane
banked high with hedgerows,
touching ninety and her thigh.
More the type to take a train,
'who's always going somewhere' (she said) 'but never
    arrives.'
Half my life's been spent,
though, in taxis; and being lifted through a lush terrain
of farms, in her 2-cv, in hers.
She even told me once my birthday meant
driving up with a hangover,
'one of last year's hangovers',
stopping at every lay-by
while I trembled on the verge.

I'm on the road again,
out on highway 61,
twenty-four hours from Tulsa –
it's a different sort of urge,
a different sort of hunger,
so they tell me: an engine's throbbing pulse.
Not where we drive, nor how far,
but what we're driven to, maybe.

Quiet Nights

Two turtles hang their heads in shame
as they go through with it, their incredible
slow-motion
mating game.
Though small and edible
they are all too human –
she sinks as low as any woman;
subsiding gently, might he not
be more than pleased with himself?
Although the ambience isn't much
on their slippery shelf . . .

We sit and make conversation
about the time your father was the star
in *West of Zanzibar*.
His second wife,
or third, went with him on location.
She took herself off
into the jungle on her own –
I want to be alone –
and tip-toeing across a standing pool
stepped on a log that moved.
The crocodile, at least, kept its cool.

Under the palm fronds, flat out
on his flat green rock
two feet from our tequilas,
the baby croc
keeps his cool too, and basks
in a never-ceasing shower,
but still cries crocodile tears.
It's not that he feels unloved –
to live the literary life
for an hour
is all he asks . . .

Your mother was photographed here
in a zebra-striped dress,
her mouth a blackened O
in a crowd of brilliant smiles, the year
you were born. No more no less
a baby
than when you were picked up by the Sheikh
of Araby.
You called it rising from the debris.
You looked like Bardot
in *Le Mépris*

or something in a cage
as you padded round your open-stage-
set studio off the Bayswater Road
in style, in things you'd never worn
till then,
or answered a crazed caller just after dawn
by screaming, naked, at the door.
I cowered behind you, squatting like a toad
in a frozen lake
of its own jissom,
shivering, thinking my time had come.

I wasn't so far wrong. Trying to fit
any kind of life together
with you was heavy weather –
first in the do-it-yourself destruction kit
we found our spirit-level,
quart after quart
straight up and on the rocks,
orange juice, tomato, tonic, lime,
Italian vermouth.
We always had time
for just one more . . .

By midnight you'd be in tears,
saying 'I don't think you'll make it
for *years* yet. If you ever do'
– and instead of trying to pour
oil on those troubled waters
I'd have cheerfully replied
with a terse
upper-cut to the jaw,
a decisive, almost dandified
patter of left hooks
to your nose or your mouth.

Remember all the nights
I could have put everything to rights
if I'd been a little more sober, if
you hadn't talked me into one last sniff?
The paper-thin
walls of our flat in w.11
still have ears –
for the Stones, Tom Waits, Warren Zevon,
for your high-pitched laughter,
our quarrels
that sounded like nothing on earth.

They wear the scars of battle
like jewels – diamante from a glass
(for once, with nothing in)
I flung at you, that missed,
flecks of amethyst
from the coffee I offered
at fifty miles per hour . . .
Then the making up, rebirth after
rebirth.
One of us, or both, should wear laurels –
if the past counts for anything at all.

The time of my time now,
the eleventh hour.
Tequila in our wet kisses,
a salt taste as my mouth
slips and slides over yours,
my throat on fire with each swallow,
a final stiffening tang.
From Mexico
to the Carolinas
you tilt a bottle any way it pours,
salt and lemon on the back of the other hand.

A sleight of tongue.
You told me. I've never been
so far south
that all I saw was desert, cactus-land.
And now you come on as strong
as Jessica Lange
simmering nicely in her roadside diner,
so that even the barman tips me the wink
as he takes a bottle from the shelf,
grinning to himself
when I call another drink.

The Feather

She would put her heart
into a *tranche d'agneau* or Peking duck,
then while the others were letting themselves go
with a Stilton, say, or a *tarte aux pommes*
she would make her usual excuse,
get out a feather
and tickle herself pink.
At the first swallow
back would come an avocado mousse.

The rest would follow
with all the inevitability of art.

One day, as luck
would have it, the feather slipped down
her throat
as easily as a mouthful of *Beaumes
de Venise*. It cut such a swathe
through the coiled miles of her insides,
those pretty *tripes à la mode de Caen*.
When it came up against her womb
it cut right through it.

She has nothing now to fear
from the mirror with its tell-tale
little-girl-wounded stare,
the lunar tempest
and its capricious tides,
her flesh's lovely, contoured swoop and swell.

*

Before dinner you took down and read
The Unbearable Lightness of Being.

Turning from the sink
I saw my father's
just-shaved lawn
one summer morning
when I was eight,
a little pile of feathers
in the centre, a few artfully scattered
as in Dubuffet's portrait
of Monsieur Plume.
Our cat stretched out
on a sunny patch, licking his lips.

We're through with starling *Véronique*
for another week. I peel and portion
a tangerine and spit the pips

and feel the drunkenness I usually feel
when you take the bones from my plate
and crunch them up in your marvellous teeth —
leaving not so much as a splinter.

You smile at me. We climb to bed.
Cat's-eyes. Cat-slink.

Confidence

'Some of them are pearls, my friend would say,
or there are pearls in there somewhere,
for certain, if you can only find them.
And there was something else he said:
You shouldn't ever throw a pearl away.
But I've never been one for that kind of talk.

She was well known around the bars.
She was known, mostly, for that look of hers —
nothing you could really point to —
that put you in your place. It'd flare up,
kind of sudden, and there you'd be,
wondering what you'd said. No guy thinks
that he can take too much of that,
but I can tell you, there were plenty.
Most of them she wouldn't give the time of day.
A hat? Oh sure, she wore a hat.'

A Short History of Snakes

I
While the pavements throb and sweat
with summer, a steady thumping beat,
you parade and sway and stalk

about the room, a high-heeled, low-hipped walk
from drinks-tray to icebox and back.

From the record-player
come the sounds of swampland or bayou
and also on the air
the reek of dope
curls up like snake-charmer's rope.

Stretched in your armchair,
basking, his tail
in Florida, the forks
of his tongue
in South Carolina, or Texas,

is the Coral Snake –
the one who comes out at night
to bare his single tooth,
his poison fang;
or it might be the Copperhead,

coiled and coloured like a length of wiring,
his noise easily taken for a rattle,
who is 'inoffensive, retiring',
who devours
'whatever is available';

or the Cottonmouth,
the sluggish one, at home
in slow-moving waters, whose bite
'is quite likely to be lethal',
going through his threat-

routine . . . *Don't you ever make such a bad mistake,*
I'd rather fall into bed with a rattlesnake –
the very thing that makes her rich
makes me poor . . . And like a squaw
of the Iroquois, or Sioux,

you will eat,
for cunning, the flesh of the pit-viper, raw.
Don't let that woman make a fool out of you . . .
You can still see the quick nerves twitch,
there is more.

2

It has all gone like a dream,
or so it would seem –

a few drinks, of course,
a few faltering steps on the dance-floor,

his groin pressed tight to yours,
his mouth full of your hair.

A taxi through rain-shining streets.
Then the nightmare

of splintered
glass, a shard

held to your throat
as he puts you through it,

your telephone blaring, off the hook,
a drunken voice on the intercom,

a round spy-hole of light
in the steamed-up window.

The pacing of your neighbour
who is haunted, even now,

by the fact that he mistook
your final, blood-curdling scream

for the noise you often make
when he urges you to come.

*

You wake
in a tangle of sheets,

reach for the familiar, hard
flesh beside your own –

something is there
(though you cannot feel a single bone),

curled around its head,
scaly, rustling, wet.

Without a word,
he slithers out of bed

and down the stone
stairs, stops to light a cigarette.

Amarillo

Instead of the rented villa
where you stayed wide open to all comers
through one whole summer,
I'd have you take a holiday in Amarillo.

*'It's like livin' on the San Andreas
fault. Somethin' bad's gonna happen here.'*

The miles of perimeter wire
through a prairie heat-haze.

The biggest slaughter-house in Texas.
The biggest whore-house.

You'd make yourself at home
with a thirty-megaton bomb.

Red dust. Tumbleweed. An ill wind.
And a portion for the foxes,

Mr and Mrs Fox, that is.
Your unusually warm, wet lips.
She'd have to get to grips
with them piecemeal.

I'd have him go off like a rocket
over your rare pink veal
and béchamel,
then watch the rot set in.

Pièces Froides

(Satie)

Your dress is the green of an electric current
passed through a gin-and-lime
or mint
julep.

Cigarette, Famous
Grouse
disappear in next to no time

as if by a kind of osmosis
while I gulp
my second in amazement.

*Nous ne connaissons ni crainte
ni fureur*
though your limbs,
wiry,

taut and slim
as jungle grass,
have taken on
a life of their own –

your fingers waving ·
like fronds
in a palm-house.

Whatever you are saying
makes us both lean forward,
your boyfriend frowns

and the *Pièces froides*
are ice at the bottom of each glass,
a silence, then a chink that glows
hard and fiery.

A Night at the Opera

With Lafcadio Hearn
in St Pierre,
a Jean Rhys heroine –
you might have been drenched in lava –

or with the boys in the band?
He tightens his cummerbund
like Nelson thinking of Emma Hamilton,
the cock strutting with his hens about the walks . . .

(No-one noticed anything other than queer
about Sir Phineas ffox,
never slow to rise
for his best friends' wives'
levées . . .)

All through the second act
of *Pelléas et Mélisande*
she held my hand
captive between her thighs,

the whole box
growing steadily warmer.
Any port in a storm!

(Nor were we exactly
ships that pass in the night
when we discovered the English Harbour,
where Nelson might have made a last stand –
She'll triumph in my fame, or weep over my grave –

ate a lobster and went on
to market-smells of guava,
plantain, pawpaw, passion-fruit.)

From the Album

Your flounces settle, fall away
from here to Algeciras,
shivering in her power . . .

In the mountains,
there you feel homeless, unhappy and afraid.

The Rif in Tarifa, the whiff of a *grifa* –
the Atlas quartered
under my raised hand, one wide gaze
takes in the whole of Africa.

A cauldron of unholy loves.
And we are at the usual villa,
the afternoon ripening through orange groves,
cactus and bougainvillaea,

arbours and balconies and room and shade . . .

From an open door off that Moorish
courtyard,
the whispering of a shower
like the Alhambra's million fountains.

You're lying low. Whorish
tricks on a sofa, someone
hisses sweet nothings while
you take him in.

You'll be wearing white,
keeping it close to your skin . . .

You, your mother and myself,
together for one photograph –
two of us glowering against the light,
you the only one to smile.

Sub

She knows exactly what you're trying to say
and wants to save you from yourself.
There's this problem, nothing really, of a Latin tag.
And did you really mean Pythagoras?

You have it sorted out by lunchtime.
She's off with some fifth columnist –
her mouth comes to grips
with buttered-up asparagus,
then attacks a plate of *insalata mista*.

Mid-afternoon, she may come back
with a streak of Farah
Fawcett. Her black
Mini disappears into traffic
along the Embankment . . .

Dinner, and the low-down on her day.
Another drink, and then another drink.
Stepping from her doorway
and through the bookshelf
you find her in the pink –

sheets. Pillows. Duvet. Bathroom tiles.
A toothpaste-smear.
Her laundry-basket's frill of handkerchiefs,
the A-cups
of her bra. Bikini-briefs.

And the oh-so touching mouse's tail
that snakes out of her mat of hair
or curls in its own furrow
between two white half-moons. The cusp.

Marilyn and You

From one of her sky-high heels, Marilyn
would lop off
a quarter of an inch,
a horse-shoe in miniature,
so that she could toe the line
the more unsteadily
between insanity and lunch,
or walk a high-tension wire
she could never see the end of
(they always gave her too much, or too little rope);
she went skeetering, all ass-wiggles,
hip-swayings, thigh-jiggles,
down a shocking slope
to the bed where they found her jack-knifed.

Photographs would have her looking well-dressed
in black high-heels
and not much else.

You wear yours to parties – that little lift –
and only look unsteady when you're drunk, or bored
off-balance.
You've never used them to pin any part of a man

to the floor, or stamp a military tattoo
on his chest.
I've seen them flung anyhow in the cupboard
among the bras and pants
and given them a second glance.
I've watched you, after half a mile, totter
and almost fall. Go barefoot rather than.

Politics

Mid-afternoon, just in from lunch,
he will stop ostentatiously
in front of your desk
and say, to no-one in particular,
What have I got to do
to get that on the end of my prick?
That evening, over a drink or two
with your steady boyfriend,
you won't know who he thinks he is . . .
when another will sit down, grip your haunch
behind everybody's back
and suggest that you two meet later that week,
for dinner, *and some fun afterwards* –
in those, or in so many words.
Your boyfriend will agree that it's grotesque.
He'll wonder where it will end.

It ends in a room with a single naked bulb,
your naked body they will stretch
between electrode
and switch.
On it they will etch
a map of desire.
And will you be the more betrayed

by whimpers, shouts, the steady trick-
ling of yourself onto the floor,
or – when one of them, sucking ostentatiously
on the remains of a joint and extinguishing the rest
just below your left breast,
slams back the bolt
of a hand-gun he has slid,
cold inch by inch, half-way inside –
by your involuntary spasm of diarrhoea?

Isabel

Two hedonists fellow-travelling
from history to food
and back – it's all a cat's cradle
or a spool unravelling – will pause
and gaze at the forum
while the cats multiply
and swarm
like ivy over the stones,
savage, harum-scarum
scavengers at play.

Could even Miss Archer
have found them hateful?
She might have adjusted her stance,
without the slightest risk to her poise –
but what of this one, nose-up, scenting fish-smells,
picking airily
along the shoreline,
deftly turning clams, cockle-shells
to turn up the odd head of a sardine
on its claws?

And you had flown in from Buenos Aires,
Riva Schiavoni or New York
to toy with your mood –

a baffled, not ungrateful
dissatisfaction with life –
at the end of your knife
or dangle it
on the end of your fork,
pick over your future
in the entrails of a trout.

Le Var

When he thinks of that time now
he thinks of going under, X that marked the spot,
or coming round to the stink
of his own insides; the sweat of his brow
that a girl mopped
with tears in her eyes, remarking how he made
no more impression on the sheet than a shade;
through blinds the neon blinking on and off: *Hôtel* . . .

*

He looks. He looks hard
at the farmhouse in a rubble-scattered yard,
at the black tooth-gaps of missing slates,
a moped
propped against the metal gates.
Muddied standing water
coming to the boil in its own sewer-smell.
Défense d'entrer, défense

d'entrer – outbuildings, sinks, taps and tiles,
a rusted mill-wheel's creaking silence,
a rustle of bamboo.
An ambush. The sudden high-pitched squawk
of birds in a flap, the whole flock
darkening the air – and, not five yards away,

the huge slumped cow's dead weight,
its legs stiff and splayed,

a trickle of black on its stomach
and from both nostrils, eyes
like something seen by Rimbaud.
A buzzing veil of flies
drawn over piles of purple-reddish stuff
in a corner, piles of gristly yellow-white.
It is so dream-still and hot
he will stand there hours.

*

She is trussed, naked, in a kitchen,
confessing all. The howl of an Alsatian
in the hills, headlights on the road to Marseille.
An engine backfiring, a shot, maybe,
in the dark. Black water closing over quicksand
at the quarry where they slaughter
cars – a Merc and a Citröen,
bullet-starred, rusting in the *maquis*.

Under the Influence

Waking to first heat like an oven-blast,
the chirring of crickets, thyme and rosemary smells –
the terrace is a scatter of deckchairs and glasses
and L.P. sleeves, a drowned wasp circles slowly
in an inch of cognac, and the deaf-mute cook-
housekeeper mimes a surly *bonjour*, frowns
and clears dinner-plates from under piles
of butt-ends, crushed cigarette-packs, coffee-grounds
and crusts. I barely glance up from my book
when the hosts come down, all smiles . . .

I read, *The consul felt a clutch at his heart*;
if you had sent the postcard
he slips under his wife's lover's pillow,
if you came back, now (although *the case is altered*),
dreaming of *the cabin between the forest
of pine and high, high, waving alders*,
could I reach for you simply, seeing as if with eyes open
again, drinking in your hurt gaze,
or should I reach first
for the bottle of mescal, of bourbon?
Mid-morning heat, a hangover, *eau gazeuse* . . .

Our mad captain will attack
the mountain, the abandoned farmhouse at daybreak.
Alone by the swimming-pool in total dark
I murmur, *For Christ's sake,
for sweet Jesus Christ's sake, come back*.

Guardian Angel

   (from Cattafi)

A cat-house in Tunis. I'd barely
put a foot inside the door
when they asked me was I a sailor? No I said
but I might as well be,
I get around so much. Whoever
gets around that much
takes everything with him, including fever.
Three girls were buzzing around the room –
une Française, from Lille, as it turned out,
an Italian bit, and the third,
an Arab, very swarthy –
from Oran –, the best.

You're sick, you've got a fever,
the eyetie piece informed me
and she seemed to think that the last word.
I asked her how the hell she could tell –
you can see it in your face, she said, you're burning up
and in your eyes, she said, you
can see it everywhere.
You're completely off the wall, I said,
you don't know me from Adam, and anyway,
since when can you tell what goes on
under a person's skin?
But she just brushed my forehead with her palm
and the fever went up ten degrees at least.
Clear out, she said, it's
your health I'm thinking of, I'm
your guardian angel. Well
thanks but no thanks I answered
you can leave me out of all that, so far
you've only made things worse.
I made a move for Khedidja, the girl from Oran –
the angel, who was white as the driven snow,
flushed deep red,
put a big breast
back inside her slip, and hit me
right between the shoulderblades
with these words:
You're digging yourself a grave
with your own two hands.

Or Would You Rather Not Be Saved

That night I turned up at her place soon after nine –
the friend of a friend, I had the usual contacts –
two girls were waiting. That was the first surprise.
The next came after some chaste chat of this and that

when the conversation took a turn for the worse
and the way they handled the vodka martinis
left me reeling, trying to explain
a morning glory. They'd never heard. They laughed
as I trotted out the half-remembered facts,
the bladder filling, the all-important nerve,
the pressure, the inevitable rise.
Another drink? Sure, why not. I talked with verve
and a handful of nicely-balanced ironies
about the flattery such simple unconscious acts
as turning to someone, on waking, could imply –
I was telling this against myself, of course,
for how else should they interpret my sudden shaft
of half-feigned bitterness? And that was why,
when I sank back and saw both pairs of eyes on mine,
the eyes and the air between us seemed alive
with expectancy, or hope. A light acid rain
fell on the windows, the ticking of clocks
filled a split second's silence, and the hive
in my head buzzed with the usual swarm
of memories, dream-like adrenalin-administered shocks
at the forms desire can take, when it takes form.

Were we going out? We were. A moment later
we hit the street. The pavement was a sidewalk,
not a pavement, so I knew we were in New York.
It struck me that rather than use my given name
they both referred to me as Mickey Finn.
They seemed to find that amusing. *Would it be McCool?*
I settled for *You can call me Al.* It sounded lame.
We reached a bar, all three of us (the friend
seemed to be along for the ride). Both were pretty,
one of them, dark and sloe-eyed, hardly spoke
while the other, blonde, aggressive, witty,
turned everything, herself included, into a joke.
I was already in two minds, so sat down

between them, and after a while – if I'd dared to look
it would have been as obvious as an open book –
a slim hand came to rest tattoo-lightly on each thigh.
And stayed there. Something stirred. I was trying to focus
on a tiny ear-ring that winked and flashed from a waiter
(and, at the same time, to catch the barman's eye
for two fresh marguaritas) when the floor
came up to meet me, the ceiling went into a spin
and the walls began to fly apart.
They helped me to my feet. I tottered. *Crazy*
limey sons-of-bitches, lousy motherfuckers
was the judgement muttered by the barman
backed up by something that was half-grimace, half-frown
as I staggered off and through a swinging door
leaving him to entertain Dolores, nickname Carmen,
and Faye, also known, apparently, as Daisy,
with his tale of how a guy named *Lionel . . . Lionel . . .*
Johnson, from New Jersey, some place like that . . .
had died by falling from that same high stool.
A hat? Oh sure, he always wore a hat.

I swayed down a corridor I thought would never end
and into a rose-garden I'd never hoped to enter –
music flowed out from a fountain in the centre
like water from a rock – 'Drugs, alcohol, little sister' –
and at every turn I stumbled on a vista
that for elegance outdid Versailles or Vaux;
a bowery chamber wherein at last I sate
gave on Niagara Falls, the Empire State,
and the Golden Gate Bridge, San Francisco.
It was there I almost left my heart.
In fact I just managed to keep it to myself
and by the time I staggered out, having said goodbye
to the drinks, the taco chips, an olive or two
the fountain had gone, the roses also, and the only view
was of a tiled wall, a mirror, some basins and a shelf
that ran along it. I loosened my tie,

dipped and cupped my hands, brought them to my face
as though these were the last drops of water on earth.
Straightening up, I looked myself straight in the eye –
or meant to, for what I saw in its place,
rising from the depths of the glass, was this:
the familiar eyes, the pink-rimmed smile, a trace
of cruelty in the lines of the mouth, blowing me a kiss
and beckoning me down a passage lit like a tomb
that I might have seen before. The lips moved
and I heard these words: *I see your health's improved.*
Listen now to what I say, for what it's worth.
You know I've made the chandeliers in this room
shake with laughter, and looked long and deep
in this huge mirror down one wall. You know
already what's been done to me, and by whom,
on this carpet or that bed,
and once upon a time, at this table, I spread
two crooked lines, one of heroin, one cocaine.
All that's over and done with now.
The numbers in my book, the shrill prr-prr
from the telephone, are useless as the row
of party dresses you often flicked through,
the miniature Manhattan on the shelf,
the books and records thrown on one collapsing heap,
the shoes and nylons spilling from a drawer.
Do you still think of me, of what we were?
One day I'll wake up on a cold bare floor,
past all pain, feeling not quite myself.

The lips faded like a faintly glowing ember
and others now appeared where they had been.
They tried to work themselves into a smile
then writhed and spat. *I'm the party queen*
of avant-garde New York, and London too. Remember?
You ought to. You looked me up in my hotel,
took me to dinner, and I made it worth your while.·
I guess you could call this my season in hell.

That's Ram-bo. You know, like Rambo Reagan.
An evil enchanter of the world. I'm stoned again.
But it's not my fault. First they'd spike my drink,
and then spike me. I've felt so many pairs of hands
getting in on the act, and after so many one-night stands
I've come round, vaguely, to the beast with two backs,
or woken from a nightmare to its stink.
Even when I slept two to a room,
chatelaine of my elect society,
I couldn't keep out a third, pushy member.
He wore suspenders, fishnet stockings and mascara
and must have known my reputation for sobriety.
The noise he made all night, trying to come
woke my room-mate – getting used to the dark
she stared, fascinated, at my hurry
to fan, with my own hand, a live spark
from that dead or dying ember.

I was beginning to wonder what kind of club
I was in – it would have been known to Groucho Marx,
that much was certain – when this face, too,
dimmed slowly and went out. All I'd heard
had materialized before me, every word –
on the mirror, in a lipstick-scrawl.
I was about to go through it once again
when there swam lazily into my ken
these brown baked features – a corpse, almost,
so tightly were they drawn, or an actual ghost –
that seemed to have burnt up from within,
a map of torments printed on the skin.
I thought I knew him, but all the same shrank back.
I was a writer once, he said, *a bit like you.*
(I could have said he taught me all I knew.)
I suppose I looked for inspiration in the sack –
or myself. But this is no time for smalltalk.
You'll want to know how I got to be this way

and how the writing comes to be on the wall.
Maybe when you've heard what I have to say
you'll make a note of it. There have always been messages
scribbled, in the morning, in lipstick, on mirrors.
That time, it was the usual comedy of errors –
the pick-up (he looked snug in his denims, street-wise),
the cocktails, the poppers, a shower and massage,
the two-hour acrobatics – man, that boy could fuck –
the pillow-talk and sleep-drenched eyes.
Right enough, I'd not believed my luck
but when I woke, it seemed my luck had changed:
I reached for him, but while I'd dozed
he'd taken off, my wallet with him, I supposed.
Well, it hadn't. But when I went into the bathroom
I entered a different dream, one that still goes on –
he'd been jacking up, and had opened a vein,
and was slumped, still naked, on the john,
blood everywhere, and on the mirror, his bright red daub
smeared with a finger: WELCOME TO THE AIDS CLUB

With that, a stem of pain shot through him;
he winced, trembled like a heatwave
and faded. Nor did I take my leave
less swiftly. I was shivering like an icy fire,
cold sweat ran off my limbs and torso
as I groped my way out of the door, a-
long the purple passage with upholstered walls
and back towards the restaurant, the barman,
to Faye or Daisy or (had I heard her saying?) Cora,
to Dolores, also known as Carmen.
I thought I'd been gone two hours or so
but no-one took much notice – they were higher
than a pair of kites, or two kids still in college –
as I sat down. Someone was singing,
Do you want to go to Heaven, or would you rather not be
    saved?

We all agreed we'd had one too many highballs,
so how about some food? It came. We sat and ate.
Avocado salad. The salmon of knowledge –
the raw and the cooked – on everyone's plate.
A bottle or two of California Chablis.
I must have been carried out on a stretcher
and felt about as popular as Wild Bill Hickock
at the Crazy Horse, or an SS uniform at Rick's.
After that things are a little sketchy
but the yellow cab showed ten dollars on the clock
and there was an odd scent that reminded me
of a trip to Honfleur, Rouen, Nîmes and Nice,
the Ile St Louis: ten years – all Annie's –
were on the clock, the clock had stopped, the cabbie
looked askance as though to ask what kind of bum
would leave a girl that way, and what a girl,
Second Avenue was running like the Styx
as we poured ourselves inside and back upstairs,
I was murmuring about the rooftops of Paris
in the early morning, alabaster breasts in a wide bed,
a jet-black triangle, dripping, stepping from the shower
and a towel wrapped like a turban round her head
when my companions shrieked *Paris? Is that Paris, Texas?*
Would you be a desert heart? and we had all come
to ourselves in another dimension – theirs.
Someone was making a commotion in the next world
or in the next room down the hall – *A girl needs a gun*
these days on account of all the rattlesnakes –
a joint was in my hand, I talked for an hour
about the yeti, a shy beast, born of rejection,
and drank the bitter coffee that bubbled in the kitchen
until the theme was exhausted, there was nothing left to do
but sink deeper into the scatter-cushions,
watch half-comprehending while they kissed
(I'd never seen so many uses for a tongue, or lips),
whispered and giggled softly – *How like you this?* –

and toyed with each other's earlobes and hair
so that by the time they sidled out, hip to hip,
hands resting gently on each other's shoulders,
I was about two thousand years older,
I was looking for a lost key, an old place, I was there
already, they were seeping from my touch –
it really didn't seem to matter over-much –
in that dark wide realm where we sleep with everyone.
The next thing after the next thing I knew
the sheet they'd draped over me like an afterthought
was inching its way down my body, taut
with fear, or perhaps it was merely apprehension;
in the waning darkness I could make them out,
standing to left and right, naked, each holding one corner
and holding themselves, with their free hands,
in a state of extreme creative tension;
I tried to move, but was held by invisible bands,
by the arms of Mary Jane, Mary Ann or Mary Warner,
by the gaze of Daisy, the glories of Dolores –
as well as mine, that everything now pointed to,
that, it was clear, my short immodest stories
had, in their eyes, fallen far short of;
unable to contain myself, I was on the rack
and pointed my own accusing finger back.
This must be my come-uppance. *Are they for real?*
was just about the only thing I thought of.
To this moment I can't say. I needed rest.
I watched the light come up in the west
over fire-escapes, trellises, brick, iron and steel,
the last stars going out; got up and dressed
and walked the five blocks back to my hotel,
my eyes fixed on the tattooed star on Dolores' breast,
on the down that dusted Daisy, her dorsal swoop and swell.

Crab

Above their miniature promontories
the gulls circle, circle,
or swoop
to grow fat on fish-heads. Easy pickings . . .

This late sun greys everything –
water, chain-printed mud,
cliff-wall and the Harbour View Hotel
are made of one metal.

Down at the rocks
a small boy
picks his way,
ankle-deep in yellowish scud,

then hunkers over
his wobbly reflection in a pool
to look right through it:
weed like girls' hair,

the rust-red blobs
of anemone, cut-throat
cuttle-bones, barnacles
like coolies' hats.

He puts a hand
into that clear soup
to lift a pebble,
and sees the crabs

scuttle sideways, carrying their backs.
It is terrible,
how quickly they are gone
in a swirl of water,

a puff of sand.
Starfish, rank urchins,
dried sea-things
collect on a shelf

in the kitchen where
a crab is dressed for dinner,
and I stoop
once more, while there's time, to lose myself.

Imagine My Mother Dancing

or stopping in the nursery late at night.
She will appear in pearls and a new fur,
*a cloud of perfume and a burst of light
from a diamond hair-clip*. That's her,
pouring cocktails from a silver shaker
into a glass like an upturned parasol, glancing
at Daddy. Imagine her dancing,
looking over someone's shoulder for a sign
from him – that he's watching her, that he thinks
she's beautiful . . . How her eyes shine,
something to do with all those drinks,
with memory. Stubbing cigarettes in the sand,
pursing her lips for the lipstick/mirror, taking my hand
and drawing me to her suddenly in a crowd
out shopping one afternoon, laughing too loud
at Daddy's jokes. *Imagine my mother dancing.*

Biographer

For this, our final heart-to-heart
you meet me in a room by the sea,
the floor almost underwater,
a single kerosene lamp.

As we step outside, the salt spray
stings our eyes. You say,
I dreamt the war was still going on.
The whole thing makes me so damn tired . . .

You decide to make a run for the border
from where you will travel steerage on a tramp
for Madagascar, but fetch up in Marseille.
Papers, for once, in order.

As always, there is the part
I'll need to rewrite,
your saying you wished you could be left alone,
the rest drowned by surf slapping at the wall.

Last seen in a bar
on the Canebière
by now you might be anywhere,
if you are anywhere at all.

Sorting

Back in the room you called your den:
a whiff of gas, of varnish, turps,
old rags and rust. Piles of papers,
letters, cuttings, drawings, then
the box of ribbons, buckles, medals, shells —
sorting them, I'm in your element, remote
from literature, my mummy's-boy self . . .
The German fighter-pilot's leather coat

that always hung behind the door
except on bonfire afternoons – I wore
it through my teens, and loved its smells
of leather and tobacco, its lining flecked
with whisky-stains; the collar I turned up
like a '40s hero, laconic and aloof
(ripped seams, ruined patches proof
of my ten years' neglect . . .)

These must be sorted too: the shelf
of green- and orange-covered Penguins, Conrad,
    Maugham,
Simenon (she still calls upstairs –
Your supper's nearly ready. Mind you keep warm –
and sings 'Bali Hai' to the cats). For forty years,
you dreamt of folly like Almayer's.
Foxed pages, bindings disintegrate.
Pipes. Fishing tackle. You were more like Maigret.

Ties

The dark green Tootal with white spots he wore
in the first photograph of him I saw –
the tie he lent to me for my first date

and later told me I could keep,
the matching scarf too. So 1930s,
I might as well have been in the war.

Two autumn-coloured, large-check ties
that gave me, so I thought, the air
of a schoolmaster out of Evelyn Waugh.

Then the red houndstooth, a bracing affair
with a dash of gin-and-it or *Brighton Rock*,
a lounge-lizard's whiff of the paddock.

The last, that I've worn once, I took
because I had to: black, a sort of crêpe
he bought for funerals, and hated.

The Seal

Five minutes from my flat, that you never saw, the canal-side
walk I never had the chance to take you on. Yesterday, I
looked back down the towpath as a kayak twitched under a
bridge, its wake all glint and dazzle; moments later, it slid
by, as soundless and purposeful as an arrow on the water,
oar-blades flashing in an effortless figure-of-eight, a boy's
bright orange back tensed and upright as a board – fifteen
years ago, twenty, the boy might have been myself . . .
When, already middle-aged, you could finally afford your
own ramshackle, twin-berthed fishing boat, you kept it
moored in a nearby yard, and every week-end you'd go off
to work on her hull – soft patches everywhere, you said – or
tinker with her pumps and steering gear, then sit in the pub
and swop stories with the houseboat crowd. One Saturday
you turned up to find only the top of her tiny deckhouse
showing above water – a length of driftwood, waterlogged,
ungainly, nosing through shoals of rubbish, nudging a
gorse-grown bank and pushing off again, had found the one
soft patch you'd not yet fixed. You didn't speak of it much,
or only to make a joke for the same houseboat crowd you'd
still, occasionally, drink with. I think of it only now,
remembering your skilled hands at the delicate operation of
fitting the rudder, or tightening bolts on the oil-slimed
engine, your face all concentration. I remember, too, the
time when, one summer holiday, we'd borrowed a friend's
boat to tack up and down an estuary, and ran aground, the
keel grinding sickeningly into a mud-bank – as we sat, the
sheets slack in our hands, you frowning and joking by turns,

saying the tide would float us off but worried that the light would only last an hour at most (breezes plucking at the mainsail, a rippling, flapping signal of *ennui*), a seal came by, indolent, attractive, so close we could see her startled eye and wide spindrift gaze toward paradise, her smooth head cleaving the water in a gentle V, the scroll of her wake; so unhurried we watched her for a full five minutes.

My Father's Winters

Flushed, unfussed, unreluctant, dapper,
you masterminded the bonfire, the Guy, the catherine
    wheels.
I came trotting at your gum-booted heels
when you strode up to light the blue touch-paper
and retired, suddenly a silhouette
drawing on the umpteenth cigarette.

Or you'd hang around in your duffle-coat
being one of the boys, diffident
and smiling, buying rounds from the pub that didn't close
all night, while I stamped and froze
and clutched a hot dog, a cup of soup,
watching the Regent Street lights go up.

It was snow you hated most, and there was snow
the day we burnt you; and a week or so
after, the neighbours had a mass said for you
though you hated all religions too –
snow on the church, the crib, the shepherds and kings,
like a blueprint I found among your things.

The year you retired for good, you got away –
a cottage on an estuary, a friend, some booze.
In the photograph he took of your back
the sky, the mud-flats and water are the same dull grey
and you're wearing duffle-coat and boots,
looking out, scenting tar, salt, seaweed and wrack.

The Promise

Your 'just getting hold of a boat
and going off' was always a possibility,
though each year it looked more remote.
They're still there, waiting: the jetty
and an M.F.V., and the inn,
weatherboard and varnish, high stools
ranged along the bar – *The Spanish Main*,
I've seen it – waiting too. Our rooms would have
that smoke-and-whisky smell, a masculine
perfection. We'd never shave
closer than a quarter-inch of stubble, you'd perform
your favourite role, the Outcast of the Islands,
mad for rum and mescalin.
And the only real ship of fools
would bring them from Miami for the season,
paying to the hilt to chase marlin,
bewildered by our surly silence.
At night we'd be running firearms
to Cuba or Jamaica, lashing down tarpaulin,
taking money for old rope in the Keys –
you'd keep your knack of riding out the storms.

Habits

The habits that I have from him:
kneading my head with a towel after swim-

ming or a shower
for the best part of an hour,

as though my life depended on it;
shaving always from left to right,

wearing a watch on the inside of my wrist,
giving an unconventional twist

and sideways tug to each shoelace –
the kind of thing a friend might notice

and wonder why that way and no other –
or have from contrariness: the aromatic pother

I've trailed around since I was eighteen
and started smoking Gitanes,

sans filtres, which I first saw
at home, abandoned to a sideboard drawer –

they were fatter than my father's Guards,
smelt richer, odder, and left little shards

of bitterness on the tongue;
a preference for bourbon to scotch, the salt-wet tang

of oysters to herrings and eels –
anything trite or trivial –

might it be these, more than a clutch of cells,
height, nose, hands and whatever else

that lock us together, always?
Or, now that I affect his unworldly-wise

detachment, try out his bonhomie
and am as helpless as he was in the hands of money,

have I taken on board, too,
his huge fear? – that what women do,

once they've pinned up a child like a brooch,
is all reproach, reproach, reproach . . .

I am the age he was when he found a wife –
night after night, I tried to wrestle life

into a girl, shutting out the ward's white glare,
his growing tinier and more impotent there . . .

She's gone now, and I have the magazines
I found among his cartoons, English scenes

and back numbers of *Night and Day,*
Picture Post, Yachting World, The Studio –

traces of hours spent at a drawing-board
or messing about on someone else's boat:

the airbrushed '30s models for the nudes he sketched,
the later, pink and purple Vs, the legs outstretched,

the fingers busy in each burning bush.
Not one is waiting for the artist's touch,

and nothing will come of these, these tracks
like a snail's or melting wax,

a slow trickle down the length of my arm
from the cupped and milky palm.

A Version of Pastoral

We strayed into a clump of oak and beech
and everything was vernal, English –
the hills would go their own gentle ways
for ever, sheep safely graze,
stunned in their own shadows, or wander
into the wild blue yonder . . .
Then the lake. Bulrushes, statues
like Emma Hamilton striking her attitudes:
a nymph or two, a goddess, the eighteenth-century
penchant for negligées and a ceinture –
and I would not have been fazed
to see you step from behind the neoclassical façade

of the bathing-house, a towel held by your chin,
water still dripping from your flush-tinted skin
(since I had all your wonders
in that, or some other state of undress,
constantly before my inward eye)
but I saw myself, aged nine or ten, instead,
wading through the shallows with a shrimp-net
and my father, whipping up into a kind of frenzy
a hair-thin rod, waxed line, a fly –
none of this looked exactly user-friendly
as it coiled and sang around his head
like a lariat, or something spun by Lachesis . . .
I went towards him smiling, there was stasis
as a rainbow-trout flopped in a lazy arc
out of the water and back into its circle
of ripples, the spell was broken
and I was alone on the lakeside; with everything unspoken
as it always had been – I was not there for his *Kismet* –
I left us, his rod scything out as if in flight,
our eyes intent, the fly, finally, afloat.

Talking to the Undertaker

Vanessa Ayer 1937–1985

We went to see a woman with a Tarot pack,
a glass globe and a chart of the Zodiac

before we were both semi-orphaned.
She took in her own two hands, my hand,

and saw, as if it were a screen – *like
television, honestly* – in one long look

that everything would work out *in the end
between you and your friend,*

plotted my life as if
she'd read it, saw my father coming to grief,

saw *water, sunlight on an estuary,*
a steel-grey sheet *of silk or mercury* –

it was like something given
in trust, the light of every new beginning –

saw an Anglepoise tilted upwards
as if receiving light, a sheet of words . . .

With darkness by six there comes
not the odour of sunless chrysanthemums

but the unmentionable odour of death,
a rasping of breath

and the glare on each white wall
of the burning hospital,

a sheet turned down, a trace
on your mother's grave Minoan face

of a light more rich
than that to which

Caravaggio abandoned a boy in awe and fear,
more subtle than the light Vermeer

ushered gently through a window in Delft
for the marriage of dust-motes, flesh and air.

She said: *The deceased will be myself.*